CW00400605

TABLE OF CON

Your New Puppy

The first few weeks

Your complete guide to welcoming a puppy into your family.

BY EDD DAWSON

DaisyElli🐾tt

First Printing, 2018
ISBN: 978-1-9829137-9-3
Daisy Elliott Publishing
15 Foster Avenue, Beeston, Nottingham, NG9 1AE, United Kingdom
www.daisyelliott.com

Disclaimer

Although the author and publisher have made every effort to ensure that the information in this book was correct at press time, the author and publisher do not assume and hereby disclaim any liability to any party for any loss, damage, or disruption caused by errors or omissions, whether such errors or omissions result from negligence, accident, or any other cause.

This book is not intended as a substitute for the medical advice of a licensed veterinary practitioner. The reader should regularly consult a veterinary practitioner in matters relating to the health of their pets and particularly with respect to any symptoms that may require diagnosis or medical attention.

INTRODUCTION

Your New Puppy – *The First Weeks* is your invaluable guide to caring for your new companion and giving them the best start in life.

In this book you will learn:

- How to prepare yourself, your house and your family for the arrival of your puppy.
- What to expect when collecting your puppy from the breeder.
- How to introduce your puppy to his new environment and family.
- How to sleep train for quiet nights.
- The all-important toilet training skills!
- First steps in training and socialisation.
- What to feed for healthy growth.
- Healthcare considerations and what to do in an emergency.

Edd Dawson is the founder of Daisy Elliott, a leading supplier of dog products and supplements. He has years of experience with his own dogs as well as working in the pet supplies sector.

1

PREPARING

Welcoming a puppy into your home to become part of your family is a big step. However, it's one that can be incredibly rewarding and will change your life.

It's vitally important that you take steps to prepare for this change. You've already made a great start by taking the time to read through this book!

Over the course of the next few chapters, we will cover all the topics you need to think about when getting your new puppy. This will arm you with valuable knowledge to ensure you have a positive first few weeks.

PREPARING YOURSELF AND YOUR FAMILY

If you are reading this book, then you likely haven't had a puppy before, or it may have been so long since your last puppy that you're feeling the need to brush up on your knowledge.

Everyone who welcomes a puppy into their life is hoping for a wonderful, positive experience. That's certainly achievable, of course, but it's important to remember that a puppy will come to you as something of a blank canvas. It is your responsibility to mould your puppy into a happy, social and well-behaved dog over time. This takes time and effort, but if done properly means you'll be rewarded with the companionship of a well-adjusted and well-behaved companion for life.

You and your family should understand that there will be ups and downs to the process of training and living with your new puppy. You all need to be happy to put the effort in with patience and understanding.

It goes without saying, of course, that it's worth it!

PREPARING YOUR HOME

When your puppy arrives, he will have come from an environment that is probably quite basic, with few opportunities to get into trouble or cause any mess. Suddenly being unleashed into your home as it is now would be a recipe for disaster!

Therefore, you'll need to make preparations for his arrival.

HOME AREA

The most important thing is to create a home area for the puppy. This will be where you will keep him when he is first introduced to your home.

The aim of the home area is to limit the amount of mess and damage that your puppy can create until he is properly house trained.

As your puppy will not be house trained when he first arrives, you will ideally need somewhere that is not carpeted. If you don't have a non-carpeted area, look to get some kind of waterproof covering for your carpet.

The home area needs to have easy access to the outside so that you can quickly and easily take your puppy out for toilet trips.

The home area should also be where you can most easily and naturally spend a lot of time with your puppy. In most cases, a kitchen or large utility room will be the most sensible place.

Whichever room or rooms you use, make sure you secure them from the rest of the house. A baby-gate is perfect for preventing puppy escapes!

HOME DEN

The home den will be the most important space for your puppy: it is your puppy's refuge, where he will sleep and where he can retreat to in order to feel safe. Puppies like small, enclosed, preferably dark spaces. The den needs to be in a dry, well-ventilated area and not in direct sunlight if in the summer.

Many people now use dog crates as the home den. Research has shown that they are perfect for use as a home den: they create an enclosed space, they can be made darker by placing a towel or cloth over them, and they are well ventilated.

To a human, the cage-like appearance of a crate can look an awful lot like prison, but be assured that a puppy doesn't have your preconceived notions of imprisonment!

A crate will help you keep your puppy safe when you are unable to keep a close watch on him.

As your puppy will be naturally inclined to keep his den clean, it is also a great aid in toilet training (we will cover more on that later).

It is important, however, to not leave your puppy locked in his crate for extended periods of time, except at nighttime.

If you don't wish to use a crate, there are of course other options, such as puppy pens, but these come with their own challenges too. We'll assume for the rest of this book that you've gone for the crating option as most people do.

BEDDING

When your puppy is older, you will want to consider getting him a proper, comfortable dog bed. However, resist the temptation for now – puppies will chew on almost anything they can get their paws on, expensive new dog beds included!

At the breeders, your puppy is likely to have slept on only a very basic surface and for now won't require anything much more than that. The best solution at this stage is vetbed, which is cheap, comes on a roll, is machine washable and is not appealing to eat.

TRAVELLING BY CAR

You need to consider two things when thinking about travelling by car with your puppy: firstly protecting your puppy, and secondly protecting your car!

You absolutely do not want a puppy roaming free inside your car. In the event of an accident, a loose puppy could easily be thrown about, causing serious – or even fatal – injury to you, your puppy and your other passengers. Your puppy could even become the cause of an accident by getting under your feet and interfering with your driving.

There's also the less serious issue of damage caused to your car's interior by sharp puppy teeth and claws, or if he is travel sick or has an accident.

The safest option by far is to invest in a travel crate, which will keep you and your puppy safe in the event of an accident, as well as protecting the interior from puppy-related damage.

GARDEN

In most cases, the garden will be where your puppy goes to the toilet; therefore, it will need some preparation.

The first thing to consider is escape-proofing your garden. Do not underestimate a puppy's ability to find his way out! With a small garden, you can usually make the entire perimeter is secure by ensuring it is well fenced, but carry out a very good check before relying on that. Puppies can be great climbers, so make sure there is nothing that can be used as a ladder to get over fences. Hedges are no obstacle for a puppy, so you will need to put an additional barrier in place – wire fencing is great for this.

If you have a large garden, it may be easier and safer to create a smaller enclosed area for the puppy to use. You could fence a small area of the garden or make an enclosed puppy pen.

Puppies prefer to wee on grass, so if possible try to include at least some grass in any area you give them access to.

You should always supervise your puppy in the garden. They can be natural diggers, so you will want to ensure they don't try to tunnel under fences or dig up your favourite flowers.

Be sure to remove anything that you don't want your puppy to damage or pull over in any area of the garden that you give him access to.

You will be spending plenty of time outside with your puppy when toilet training, often at night, so think about whether you need to add any additional lighting (such as solar-powered garden lights). Otherwise, just make sure that a good torch is handy by the back door.

TOYS

There are three main types of toys for your puppy:

Toys for chewing – It is important for your puppy to have things to chew as his teeth develop. If you don't provide something specific, he will find something himself – most likely your furniture! We recommend a Kong as a chew toy: they are extremely chew-resistant and can be filled with food, which will encourage your puppy to chew them.

Toys for playing – Some of the very best toys for playing with your puppy are the simple, sturdy, knotted-rope types, which are very safe and which you can use to play tug of war games. There are also many types of soft or plastic toys available; however, be very careful with these, as if your puppy manages to break them and swallow pieces, you may end up with a very steep vet bill to have them removed.

Toys for training – All puppies are capable of retrieving, and you should encourage this. The perfect toy for this is a ball. Be sure to buy one that is small enough for your puppy to pick up in his mouth but too large to swallow.

FOOD

When you first bring your puppy home, it is wise to use the same food as the breeder has been, in order to minimise change and reduce the risk of digestive upsets, so check with them what type to get.

POO BAGS AND CLEANING MATERIALS

Your puppy will inevitably make a mess as he learns to toilet train, so be sure to stock up on cleaning materials and poo bags.

Just be sure not to use ammonia-based cleaning supplies, as the smell of ammonia can trick your puppy into thinking it's a regular toilet area, and so can actually make him more likely to relieve himself where you don't want him to!

SUMMARY

- Choose and prepare a home area.
- Have a home den ready – usually a crate.
- Purchase suitable bedding – usually vetbed.
- Invest in a travel crate for car journeys.
- Puppy-proof your garden.
- Purchase some toys for chewing and some for play.
- Check with breeder on suitable food.
- Stock up on poo bags and cleaning materials.

2

COLLECTING

The big day is approaching – it's almost time to collect your puppy and bring him home for the first time! Here are all the things to prepare and consider for the big day.

CHOOSING A DATE

When choosing a date for collection, avoid a clash with other big events or plans.

If you work then book a few days' holiday.

Don't plan to collect your puppy if you have any big social events planned. You don't want to have to leave your puppy home alone the day you get him.

Never collect a puppy and then take him away on holiday – he needs to be in what will be his new home and not somewhere temporary. This would also be unfeasible from the perspective of your puppy having all of his essential vaccinations, as these must be completed before you can take him out into the big wide world.

The ideal date will be one where you will be able to devote the first few days to your puppy with no other engagements or events to disrupt either of you.

WHAT TO TAKE

You should have everything you need for the journey home before you pick up your new puppy.

Dress appropriately

Don't wear your finest clothes. It's not unusual for a puppy to get travel sick, and he won't be house trained yet either. It's sensible to take a change of clothes for yourself just in case.

Car crate

You should have a car crate by this point, so make sure that you don't forget to put it in the car. On the very first journey, you may not actually use it (see more on this later), but it's best to have it there just in case.

Cleaning materials

As already mentioned, the likelihood of your puppy being travel sick or having an accident is high, especially if it's a long journey home. Be sure to pack plenty of the following:

- Baby wipes and kitchen roll or antibacterial wipes, for cleaning up mess.
- Plastic bin bags, for disposing of rubbish.
- Dog poo bags.
- Hand sanitiser.
- Old towels and newspaper for protecting your car.

It's best to be prepared for all eventualities!

What to expect from the breeder

The breeder should supply you with all the relevant documentation for your puppy, including Kennel Club registrations if he's a pedigree puppy.

If your puppy has had his first vaccinations, you should get the certificates for this, but it's not unusual to pick up your puppy before he's had any vaccinations.

Often a breeder will give you a scrap of bedding or vetbed so that your puppy will have something that smells familiar with him.

A good breeder will also provide you with a few days' worth of the puppy's normal food so that he again has something familiar.

Handling your puppy for the first time

Your new puppy is still very young and easily hurt if not correctly handled. When holding him, have one arm underneath him supporting his weight and the other around him to keep him safe.

The journey home

Your first real experience with your new puppy is going to be the car journey home. We won't beat around the bush here – this can be quite an experience for both of you, especially if it's a long journey.

You need to remember that this is the first time that your puppy has been separated from his mother and the rest of the litter. Added to the stress of separation is the fact of it being your puppy's first car journey. It's no surprise, then, that it can all get a bit much.

If possible, bring someone with you to help, either to do the driving or to concentrate on looking after the puppy. An extra pair of hands can be invaluable.

Your puppy is likely to be travel sick, and as he won't yet be house trained, it's likely that he will wee and poo too, so make sure to prepare your car accordingly. We suggest that you line the passenger footwell with a thick layer of paper and a towel and get an appropriately sized cardboard box with the top open to sit between the passenger's feet on the floor. Keep the puppy in this box with your passenger able to comfort and reassure him, and you are likely to be able to keep your new puppy's stress and anxiety a minimum.

Whatever preparations you make, do expect your puppy to howl and cry – it's a natural reaction and nothing unusual.

Be sure to have the fallback option of a crate in the back of the car to put the puppy in should he become too boisterous or start trying to escape. It's better to get home with everyone in one piece than not at all.

ARRIVING HOME

As soon as you are home, take your puppy to his designated toilet area and allow him the chance to go to the toilet. Let him have a drink (have a bowl ready outside) and see if he wants to explore the garden – some puppies will and others won't. After he's had a wee (or after a few minutes if he obviously doesn't need one), you can then take them inside to introduce him to his new home.

SUMMARY

- Choose a suitable date for collection – when you can devote all of your time to your new puppy.
- Prepare for the journey home – suitable clothing, car crate, cleaning materials, etc.
- Be sure to get all the appropriate documents from the breeder along with some of your puppy's usual food and a scrap of bedding.
- Try and bring someone else with you to help on the journey home.
- Be prepared for your puppy to cry and be sick: he's never been in a car before and it's his first time away from the litter!
- Have him go to the toilet and have a drink before taking him inside his new home.

3

INTRODUCTIONS

Your puppy is now in his new home! At this point, he is still very likely to be quite overwhelmed, so it's important not to try to introduce him to too much at once.

The first important place you should introduce your puppy to is his home den (usually a crate) and the room it's in (usually your kitchen) – that's enough for the first day or two. Resist the temptation to show him the whole house; let him get comfortable in his immediate surroundings first.

Your puppy should already have seen his outdoor toilet area when you arrived. Be sure to take him out approximately every 30 minutes to encourage him to do his business during the first few days.

CHILDREN

If you have children, they will no doubt be bursting with excitement to meet their new family member. It's vital that you explain that their puppy will be overwhelmed to start with and they must try to be calm and not over-excited with him. Younger children should especially be told that the puppy is more fragile than their toys and that they need to be gentle when stroking and playing.

If your children are old enough to carry the puppy, show them the right way to do so, with one arm underneath him supporting his weight and the other around him to keep him safe.

Also ensure that the children are introduced in the kitchen (or wherever else is the "home area" for your new puppy), rather than elsewhere in the house.

THE CAT

If you already have a pet cat, you will need to handle the introductions carefully. While dogs and cats can easily live together once they've got know each other, it's important to get the first few days right.

The best approach is to make sure that your cat's food and water are moved to an area away from the puppy for now, so the cat can enjoy some peace. Ensure the cat doesn't end up left in a situation where it cannot escape from the puppy.

Cats tend to come in two varieties: those that will be wary of the new addition to the family and those that will be quite bold. A wary cat will after a few days start to watch and interact with the puppy and, as long as they aren't trapped, will likely adapt well to the new situation. A bold cat may be more likely to take a swipe at the new puppy, which if it gets the puppy's eye can be serious. If you have this kind of cat (or discover you do when the puppy arrives), be sure to supervise the cat and the puppy carefully to start with.

Most cats can eventually learn to live with a puppy, and many actually end up as good friends.

OTHER DOGS

If you already have an older dog, then, just like your cat, you need to make sure they can escape from the puppy when they want. Generally, older dogs will take to your puppy with fewer potential issues than cats do.

Initial supervision is essential, but once your older dog realises that the puppy is a new member of the family, they will in most cases accept him.

Having accepted him, an older dog will not retaliate against a very young puppy when playing (puppies will attempt to play with all dogs). As your puppy gets older, your older dog will start to keep the puppy in line with gentle discipline if he steps too far out of line. Once your puppy is about six months old, your older dog will start to treat him like any other dog.

If you find your older dog does not warm to your new puppy after a few days and is cold or aggressive towards him, you will need to make sure that they each have their own space. In time, most dogs who live together will learn to get on.

SUMMARY

- Take your puppy out every half an hour to toilet.
- Don't try to introduce him to too much at once.
- Teach children how to safely hold and handle him.
- Take care when introducing him to other pets.

4

THE FIRST NIGHT

The first night away from his mother is a very big moment for your puppy. He will never have slept away from his previous surroundings before, let alone slept on his own.

Your puppy has to get used to being on his own for short periods of time before he reaches twelve weeks old, otherwise you run the risk of him developing separation anxiety. This first experience of being alone will be on his first night in your home.

Before leaving your puppy for the night, be sure to take him out for a toilet trip, then get him settled in his crate.

As he is unlikely to have realised yet that his crate is his new home den, he will probably start to cry once he is left alone. This is a natural reaction – he is in effect signalling to the rest of the family that he has become separated from the pack. In a few days, once he realises that where he has been left is his home den, he will stop crying. It's normal for a puppy to be left alone safely in his crate and he will be happy.

Of course, all this is easier said than done. It is very hard to resist the crying of a puppy, and your natural instinct may well be to go and comfort him. However, you must resist, as otherwise he will never learn to be by himself and this will cause many more problems in the future.

Most puppies left in this way will learn to be comfortable in their crate within three to four nights – the vast majority will do so within one week, and some even learn within the very first night.

If you do need to go and check on him, be sure to not enter the room to see him until there is a break in the crying (there will be breaks, so do wait for one). If you go to him when he is crying, he will associate crying with making you come, which means he won't to learn to stop crying.

TOILET TRIPS

You will need to give your puppy the chance to go to the toilet during the night to start with, as most eight-week-old puppies can't last through the night without needing a wee. As just mentioned, make sure that you only go to him when he is being quiet. When you do go to take him to the toilet, don't make a big fuss of him – keep it a simple in-and-out with as little noise and attention as possible. Carry him rather than letting him walk, in order not to get him excited or any more awake than you need to, otherwise he will find it harder to settle down again.

For the best results, don't let your puppy eat or drink for about three hours before he goes to bed. Puppies don't need food or water in the night, so don't leave any in the crate for him.

We will cover toilet training in greater depth in the next section.

SUMMARY

- It's a big change for him – he probably will cry to start with, but hold your nerve: he will quickly get used to it.
- Be sure to offer regular toilet opportunities to begin with.
- Don't let him eat or drink for three hours before bed.
- You don't need to leave food or water in the crate overnight.

5

HOUSE TRAINING

We have touched on elements of how to house train your puppy in the previous sections, but it's time now to go into a bit more depth on how to successfully house train him.

Remember that at eight weeks old a puppy has a very small bladder, and when he needs to go he needs to go – he doesn't have the capacity to wait very long at all. However, as he grows, his capacity will increase gradually over time.

We have to use as much puppy psychology as we can to aid the training process. The two key points in this context are that puppies hate to go to the toilet in their home den, and that they prefer to wee where they have been before.

Puppies usually need to go to the toilet at the following times:

- When waking up
- Halfway through the night
- After eating
- After playing

By combining this knowledge with judicious use of your puppy's crate, you can help build up the amount of time he can hold on before needing a wee again.

At each of the times above, take your puppy outside to the toilet area and give him the opportunity to go to toilet (this may take a few minutes). Once he has been, bring him in again and give him the freedom of the kitchen (or his home area, if elsewhere). However, if he doesn't go on that occasion, bring him back in and return him to his crate for ten minutes and then try taking him out again.

Over time, this routine will start to develop a rhythm and will help your puppy extend his capacity to hold his bladder.

When your puppy is not in his crate, it makes sense to keep him within a small area with a washable floor – the kitchen is usually perfect for this – as any accidents can then be easily dealt with.

When cleaning up any accidents, be sure not to use ammonia-based cleaning products, as these can mimic the smell of dog wee and will make your puppy more likely to try and use the same spot again.

Avoid letting your puppy onto carpets for as long as you can, for two reasons: firstly, carpets are of course much harder to clean than a hard floor, and secondly, to a puppy they provide the same sensation as weeing on grass, which puppies prefer.

Don't punish your puppy if you catch him weeing indoors. Doing so makes him much more likely to understand going to the toilet when you are around as being a bad thing, rather than associating it with the location. This can end up making him not want to relieve himself when you take him outside – just when you do want him to!

SUMMARY

- Puppies learn by experience and by outcomes.
- Puppies have small bladders, so you need to offer them regular toilet opportunities.
- As they grow, so does their ability to hold it in.
- Don't use ammonia-based cleaning products.
- Keep your puppy off carpets as much as you can to begin with.
- Don't punish him if you catch him weeing indoors – it will be counterproductive.

6

TRAINING

Dogs are remarkable animals when it comes to the variety of commands they can respond to and tasks they can be trained undertake. Just think of some of the everyday examples: guide dogs, drug sniffing, search and rescue, shepherding... the list goes on.

You are very unlikely to be looking to train your puppy to perform some of these more demanding jobs, but you will want to train him with simple rules of how to behave around the house, with your family, went out and about, and with strangers.

HOW YOUR PUPPY WILL LEARN

Dogs learn by experience and outcomes (in many ways not dissimilar to how young children learn!).

Put simply, if your puppy does something and gets a positive outcome, he will learn to do it again or do more of it. For example, if he plays with a squeaky toy and gets it to make a noise, he will learn that playing with the toy is fun and will want to keep playing with it. If he does something and gets a negative outcome, he will learn to avoid doing it in the future. So if he gets to close to a hot oven and burns his nose, he will learn not to get so close in the future. Relatedly, he may try something and find it to be boring, and so is unlikely to do it again: for example, if he tries to play with a brick in the garden and finds it doesn't do anything, he will learn that bricks are boring to play with and will leave them alone in the future.

So we have three possible outcomes:

- Good outcome – do more of this
- Bad outcome – do less of this
- Boring outcome – do less of this

REWARD GOOD BEHAVIOUR

Now we understand how a puppy works, we can use this knowledge to make sure that the good behaviours we want are encouraged. We do this by making these behaviours have good outcomes – in other words, that they lead to some form of reward.

In most cases, this reward will have to come from you, the owner. The reward could be making a fuss of your puppy or giving him a food treat. Different puppies are motivated by different rewards, so you will need to figure out which ones work best (though it's most often food-based rewards!).

Therefore, when your puppy does something you want him to do, such as sitting down when you ask him to, or sitting by a door to wait for it to be opened, reward that good behaviour. He will soon learn.

DON'T REINFORCE BAD BEHAVIOUR

Likewise, it is crucial that you do not reinforce bad behaviour. This is most often done accidentally by rewarding your puppy with attention. The most common example is opening his crate for him when he is making a noise. Always wait for him to be quiet before opening the crate, otherwise he will associate the action "make lots of noise" with the reward "crate door opened".

Wait for the behaviour to stop before engaging with your puppy.

MAKE BAD BEHAVIOUR BORING

If you don't want your puppy to jump up at you when he sees you, for example, ignore him and make the situation boring when he tries – only engage with him when he stops and has all of his paws on the ground. He will learn that jumping up doesn't get rewarded and makes you very boring.

LIMIT HIS RANGE (AGAIN!)

Part of this training process is to limit the bad behaviour that can be caused when you are not around. Therefore, make sure that your puppy doesn't have access to things you don't want him to play with and potentially damage when you are not around.

CONSISTENCY

It's important that your puppy gets a consistent message about what constitutes good behaviour and what does not. You must be consistent, and so must everyone else he is in regular contact with – this therefore means training your family on how to treat him to match how you behave.

SOCIALISATION

To ensure that your puppy is a well-adjusted member of society, he needs to undergo a process of socialisation.

When puppies are very young, they have no fear and are eager to explore and understand their world. This stage reaches its peak at around eight weeks, which is why this is the best time for puppies to move away from their mother and to begin life with their new family.

At twelve weeks, your puppy will start to become more cautious and wary of new experiences, and by sixteen weeks the window of opportunity is shut.

You need to socialise your puppy so that he will be unafraid of the everyday world. Dogs that are afraid tend to become aggressive, which is not a desirable behaviour. The more experiences you can provide your puppy with in these first few weeks, the less afraid he will be as an adult dog and therefore the less aggressive he is likely to be.

The following is a socialisation task list:

- *Handling* – Get your puppy used to be handled and groomed.
- *Children* – Make sure your puppy meets children, especially if you don't have any of your own.
- *Crowds* – Get him out and about: take him into town to see the hustle and bustle, or to a dog-friendly pub and shops that allow dogs.
- *Animals* – Make sure that any other animals (sheep, horses, cows, etc.) that he is likely to encounter are familiar.
- *Machines* – Get him used to cars, public transport, hoovers, washing machines, lawn mowers, etc.

Get your puppy out and about as soon as you can. While it's true he can't be out on the ground before his vaccinations are complete, to avoid the risk of exposure to harmful viruses, he can still be easily and safely carried on trips in a shoulder bag. Don't wait until he is ready to walk on the ground.

WALKING YOUR PUPPY

Once your puppy has all his vaccinations and has his immunity, you'll then be able to take him for his first proper walks out and about.

It's important, however, that for the first year you don't over-exert him, otherwise you will risk causing damage that will show up in later life.

The simple rule of thumb is five minutes of walking per month in age, so a four-month-old puppy should go on walks no longer than 20 minutes, a six-month-old for 30 minutes, and so on.

SEEK OUT MORE IN-DEPTH TRAINING RESOURCES

We've covered training here in the very briefest of detail. There are many great training resources to discover out there.

We would also heartily recommend you take puppy training and socialisation classes, which you'll find running in most areas.

SUMMARY

- Puppies learn by experience and by outcomes.
- Reward good behaviour.
- Don't reinforce bad behaviour – make it boring.
- Limit his range and remove objects that he could get in trouble with from reach.
- Be consistent in how your treat his behaviour.
- The socialisation window ends by sixteen weeks, so get in as many experiences as you can before then.
- Don't let your puppy on the ground in public before his vaccinations are complete.
- When your puppy does start going for walks, don't over-exert him.

7

FEEDING

There are several schools of thought on what dogs should and shouldn't eat. We aren't going to tell you exactly what your puppy *should* eat in this section, but we will give you some information on the three main feeding regimes so that you can follow them up further if you need to. We will also tell you about the foods that will harm your puppy if he eats them.

KIBBLE

Kibble is a dry dog food that comes in pellet form. You can buy it in anything from small pouches to giant sacks from supermarkets and pet shops. Kibble is easy to portion out, to store and to source.

The majority of domesticated dogs eat kibble, and it's likely that your puppy will be familiar with it when he arrives.

RAW FOOD

A growing number of dog owners are now feeding their dogs a raw food diet, the thinking being that this is closer to the kind of diet that dogs would have eaten prior to domestication.

While we don't necessarily disagree with the idea that a raw food diet could be nutritionally great for dogs, it does require much more work from the owner, in terms of sourcing and providing the right food, and it's a much messier job to prepare and feed.

If you want to learn more about the raw food diet for dogs, search for information on the RMB (Raw Meaty Bones) diet and the BARF (Biologically Appropriate Raw Food) diet for dogs.

WET FOOD

Less common now than it used to be is canned wet food, which can be purchased at supermarkets or pet shops.

It is bulkier and heavier than dried food, but it is as easy to store and is also nutritionally complete.

If your puppy isn't a great fan of kibble, then some wet food might be his thing.

WHAT TO FEED YOUR PUPPY TO START WITH

Whatever your feelings or desire on how to feed your puppy in the long term, we suggest that to start with you carry on feeding him food that he is used to. If he came to you as a kibble eater, then keep him on kibble to start. The main reason for this is that a sudden change of diet can cause diarrhoea, which can be very serious in small puppies, as well as an unpleasant thing to have to deal with around the house.

Once your puppy has settled and grown a little, you might then decide to try a different kind of diet. Make sure you start by gradually introducing the new food over a period of time.

WHAT TO GIVE YOUR PUPPY TO DRINK

Your puppy will be fully weaned from his mother when you pick him up and he won't need milk anymore. Avoid giving cow's milk to your puppy as he does not need it and it is likely to cause diarrhoea.

All your puppy needs to drink is water.

FEEDING SCHEDULE

A small puppy needs a lot of food relative to his size to enable him to grow, but his stomach size restricts the amount he can eat at any one time.

If you are feeding kibble or wet food, the packaging will let you know how much food he will need per day for his breed type/size and age.

When he first arrives, he will need his daily food allowance split into four equal-sized meals a day, up until around the twelve-week point.

After around twelve weeks, you can then split his food into three meals a day, and at around six months you can go down to two meals a day.

If your puppy eats more than his stomach can handle, he won't be able to digest the food properly and he will get diarrhoea. If you find that when trying to reduce the number of meals per day he develops diarrhoea, switch him back to more smaller meals a day for a while before trying again when he has grown a little.

WHAT YOUR PUPPY CAN'T EAT

There are some foods and food additives that are potentially harmful for your puppy, and you should take care to ensure he doesn't come into contact with them.

- *Xylitol* – a common sweetener found in many sugar-free products. It is a known toxin to dogs. It can be found in products such as human toothpaste, cakes, chewing gum, and sweets.

- *Anti-freeze* – contains ethylene glycol, which is extremely poisonous to pets.
- *Chocolate* – contains methylxanthines, which are harmless to humans but act as a stimulant in dogs and can cause fatal poisoning.
- *Grapes and raisins* – can be poisonous and cause kidney failure in dogs.

If you suspect your puppy has ingested any of the above, contact your vet immediately.

There are also a few other foods which you should approach with caution:

- *Onions and garlic* – should not be regularly fed to dogs as they contain disulphide, which over time can cause Heinz body anaemia. Some pet food does contain small amounts of onion in low doses with a very large safety margin and will not harm your dog's health.
- *Bones* – can cause injury to your dog if he ingests bone splinters that can cause internal damage to the digestive system. They are also a choking hazard. Always exercise caution with bones and dogs. We do not recommend them for puppies at all.

WHAT ABOUT LEFTOVERS?

Before the commercial pet food industry evolved, it's probable that most domesticated dogs lived on the leftovers from their human families.

Some owners choose to only feed their dogs pet foods or specially prepared dog foods. Others are quite happy to feed their dogs their scraps.

We wouldn't recommend feeding leftovers to your puppy in the first year, as the potential for stomach upsets from unusual food is probably not worth the hassle.

If you do choose to give your dog leftovers when he is grown up, take care that you are still providing a nutritionally complete diet.

DO I NEED TO FEED SUPPLEMENTS?

When your puppy is still small, you probably don't need to worry about any food supplements in addition to his standard food.

When he is grown up, you may want to consider some supplements, especially those that may help with particular breed traits, such as fish oil supplements for breeds prone to joint problems in later life.

SUMMARY

- The three main types of food are kibble, raw and wet.
- It's best to start on whatever food the breeder uses.
- Introduce new types of food gradually.
- Puppies only need water to drink.
- Feed little and often to start with, only switching to fewer large meals as your puppy grows.
- Learn all the foods and substances that are harmful to dogs.
- Avoid feeding leftovers in the first year.
- Supplements can be beneficial for adult dogs, but for puppies they are not usually needed.

8

HEALTHCARE

As with any member of your family, you will want to do everything you can to keep your puppy as healthy as possible and to learn what to do in an emergency.

While your puppy is small, he is at his most vulnerable to infectious diseases and injury. It's therefore your responsibility to try, as far as possible, to prevent him from catching these diseases or getting injured, and to seek treatment for him in the event this does happen.

CHOOSING A VET

You should take your puppy for his first checkup with a vet within the first few days of his arrival. You may already have a vet you use with other pets, but if not, you will need to choose a one. It makes sense to choose a vet who is local to you for convenience's sake. This may limit your choices, but if there are several local vets then ask friends for recommendations.

Don't worry too much about which vet to choose – if you find that for whatever reason you don't like your first choice, you can simply try another vet the next time, until you find one you are happy with. In our experience though, we've never come across a vet who wasn't totally committed to the health of their patients.

TO INSURE OR NOT INSURE?

If you're lucky enough to have a puppy who encounters no serious problems and grows into a dog with similarly good health, you'll have the fortune of not experiencing too many large vet bills.

However, veterinary procedures can be extremely costly, especially as treatment options are so much more advanced than just a few years ago.

Dogs can now be referred for advanced diagnostics such as MRI scans and for treatments such as chemotherapy and radiotherapy, all of which can involve bills running into the thousands should you wish to pursue them.

Many people now choose to insure their puppies to cover them in case the worst should happen and they need such expensive interventions. There is a wide selection of insurance options to choose from that will cover various different scenarios. If you choose to take out insurance, be sure to thoroughly check what each insurance plan offers, what it excludes and how it covers recurring or chronic illnesses. Not all insurance policies are created equal, and the cheaper ones are often quite restrictive in what they cover or have very high excesses.

At the end of the day, whether you decide to take out insurance will be a personal decision. However, be aware that if you don't and then find yourself down the line having to make the choice between whether to find the cash for an expensive treatment or to say goodbye to your dog, it can be heartbreaking.

EMERGENCIES

As we've mentioned before, small puppies are at their most vulnerable stage of life, and in an emergency they will need very swift treatment otherwise they can quickly go downhill and potentially die.

It's important that you recognise what is and is not an emergency.

You should contact your vet straightaway in the following situations:

- Your puppy is having trouble breathing or his breathing is unusually noisy.
- He has diarrhoea or sickness that does not clear up quickly (excluding mild diarrhoea when initially

moving in, from stress, or initial carsickness – as we've mentioned previously, this is can all be expected).

- He won't eat or is lethargic.
- He hurts himself or sustains any kind of injury.
- He swallows something he shouldn't have (or you suspect he has).
- He is crying for no apparent reason (so not if he is crying to be let out of his crate).
- He is limping or walking unusually.
- He has unusual discharge from the nose, ear, mouth or any other part of the body.
- He just doesn't seem to be acting his usual self or if you are concerned about him in any way.

A healthy puppy is very like a young child – he will tear around like crazy and be full of energy when he is awake, but when he is tired he will sleep very deeply and often.

If for any reason you think that your puppy is not behaving in a normal manner, do contact your vet – they would much rather be safe than sorry.

VACCINATIONS

Young puppies are very prone to certain infectious diseases, some of which can be deadly.

Different countries have different endemic diseases that can affect the local dog population. In the UK the most common diseases that your puppy will need protection from are:

- Canine parvovirus

- Leptospirosis
- Canine hepatitis
- Distemper

It's important that you speak to your vet about vaccinations to protect him from these common diseases and whether there are any others you need to consider.

Your puppy will most likely get his first vaccinations at his first checkup with the vet at around eight weeks old. These will then be followed by a second set at around twelve weeks. Prior to these second vaccinations, he will not be fully protected from common viruses that can cause serious illness and even death.

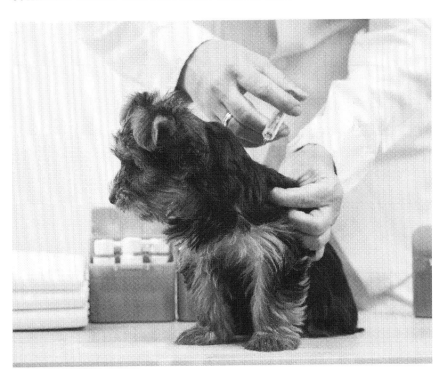

PARASITES

Your puppy should come from your breeder parasite-free and have had their initial worming treatments, but always check with your breeder that this is the case.

FLEAS, TICKS AND MITES

Don't wait for fleas, ticks and mites to infest your puppy before dealing with them – by the time you notice any infestation it will be quite deeply ingrained and could have already caused secondary issues for your puppy. The pests will also likely be all over your house, which is not pleasant for anyone.

Ask your vet at the first checkup what precautions to take to prevent infestation, such as preventative treatments that can be cheaply and easily applied.

If you live in certain areas of the country, particularly areas with lots of bracken and ferns, ticks can be a particular issue when your dog becomes active outdoors. The only safe way to remove a tick is with a tick removal tool, which you can get from any good pet store.

WORMS

To prevent worms, you will need to keep to a regular worming schedule, not only for your puppy's sake, but also for that of your family. Your vet should advise on worming schedules at the first checkup.

You should always ensure children wash their hands after handling the puppy and you shouldn't allow your puppy to lick anyone's mouth. Keep children away from any puppy toilet mess and regular puppy toilet areas.

SUMMARY

- Get your puppy registered with a vet straight away.
- Decide on whether to take out health insurance for him.
- Ensure you can recognise what is and is not an emergency.
- Get him vaccinated.
- Regularly treat with worm and tick treatments.
- If in any doubt. always consult your vet without delay.

THE FUTURE

You've made it successfully through the first few weeks with your puppy, who will by now be a happy, settled member of your family.

He's got a comfortable space all of his own, knows what is expected of him, is confident in the outside world, has a healthy diet to help him grow, and is strong and healthy.

He will soon be a full-grown dog and an integral part of your family and you will enjoy each other's companionship for years to come

Good luck and best wishes for the future to you all!

FURTHER RESOURCES

This book has been made possible by Daisy Elliott, a leading supplier of dog accessories and supplements. Visit www.daisyelliott.com for more help and advice on dog care.

DEDICATION

This book is dedicated to Moss, the author's first puppy, a beautiful, loving and devoted Flat-Coated Retriever who taught him just how much more rewarding and fulfilling life can be when there's a big hairy bundle of dog in it.

WHAT DID YOU THINK
OF YOUR NEW PUPPY?

First of all, thank you for purchasing this book Your New Puppy. I know you could have picked any number of books to read, but you picked this book and for that I am extremely grateful.

If you enjoyed this book and found some benefit in reading this, I'd like to hear from you and hope that you could take some time to post a review on Amazon. Your feedback and support will help this author to greatly improve his writing craft for future projects and make this book even better.

You can get in touch with me directly at yournewpuppy@daisyelliott.com, I would love to hear from you.

Thanks!
Edd

Printed in Great Britain
by Amazon